# WATER

John Baines

Consultants: Southern Water plc

## Titles in this series

Bricks
Glass
Paper

Plastics
Water
Wood

**Cover:** (Main picture) Water gushing over the Niagara Falls in the USA. (Top right) Windsurfers enjoying the water in Hawaii.

**Series editor:** Sarah Doughty
**Book editor:** Judy Martin

First published in 1991 by
Wayland (Publishers) Ltd
61 Western Road, Hove
East Sussex, BN3 1JD, England

**British Library Cataloguing in Publication Data**
Baines, John
    Water. – (Links)
    I. Title    II. Series
    333.91

ISBN 0 7502 0156 8

Typeset by Dorchester Typesetting Group Ltd
Printed in Italy by G. Canale & C.S.p.A.
Bound in Belgium by Casterman S.A.

# Contents

Words that appear in
**bold** are explained in
the glossary on page 30.

# We all use water

Water may seem to be a common and ordinary liquid. Pure water has no smell, no taste or colour. However water covers almost three quarters of the surface of our planet. It also makes up about two thirds of our body weight. Just imagine if there was no water. There would be no plants, no animals – no you.

Water is so common that we usually take it for granted. We turn on a tap and water flows out.

*Pulled by a boat, a water skier skims very fast over the water on a single ski.*

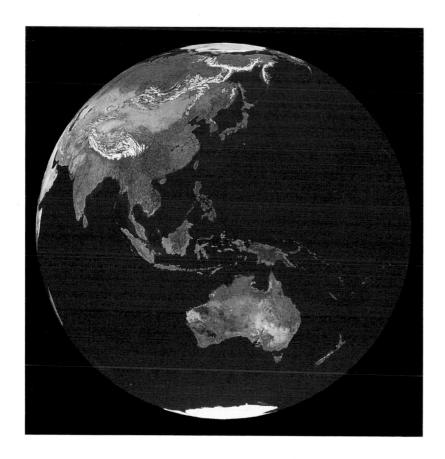

**Below** *Watering plants helps them to grow when there is too little rain.*

We use it to wash ourselves, our clothes and our dishes. We drink it, we cook with it and we flush the toilet with it. In a dry summer, we may use it to water the garden.

We also enjoy water too. People can swim in it, sail on it, and when it is frozen, skate on it. The list of the ways we use water is almost endless. In this book you will find out more about water, how people use it and why it is important.

# Water is a liquid

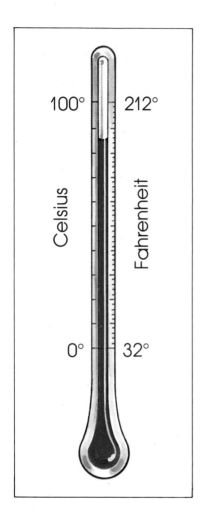

Water is a liquid. Liquids flow and have no shape. Water in a glass takes on the shape of that glass. If it is poured into another one it takes on the shape of the new glass.

When water is cooled enough it freezes and becomes ice. Ice is a solid. A solid has a shape. If an ice cube is taken out of its container, it keeps its shape until it warms up and melts to become water once again.

When water is heated in a kettle, it reaches a point at which it cannot become any hotter.

**Above** *These are the two scales we use for measuring temperature.*

**Right** *Water is a liquid that can turn into a gas or a solid.*

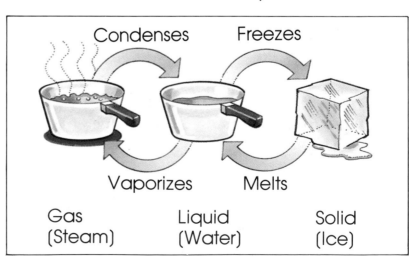

It then turns into steam. Steam is a **gas**. Gases are able to spread out in all directions.

*Large masses of ice called glaciers move slowly along valleys in cold areas of the world.*

The temperature of something tells us how hot or cold it is. We measure temperature in degrees using two scales, called Celsius (°C) and Fahrenheit (°F). Ice melts at 0°C (this is 32 °F). The temperature at which water boils and gives off steam is 100 °C (or 212 °F).

# The water cycle

Although we use a lot of water, it only runs out when there is very little rainfall. Rain brings the water that people need. But where does the rain come from?

Rainfall comes from moisture in the air. The moisture gets into the air from puddles, lakes, rivers, the soil, plants, animals and the sea. Water **evaporates** and is absorbed by the air. The air moves over the Earth as the wind and carries the moisture with it. When the air cannot hold any more moisture, it drops it as rain, snow or mist. Some falls on the oceans.

*Plants need water to grow and their leaves release water back into the air. These cotton plants in the USA are dying from lack of rain.*

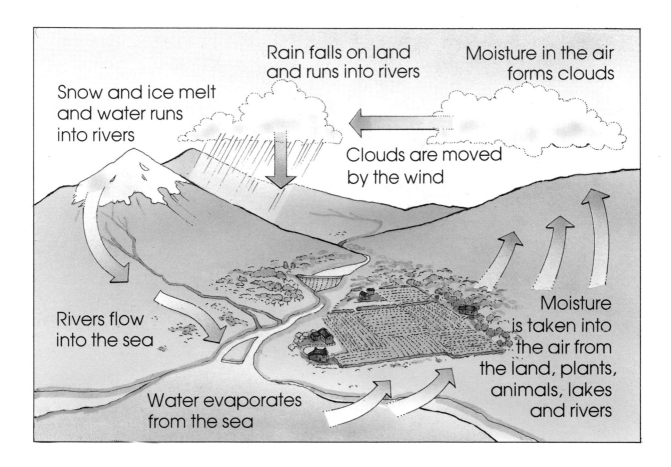

Snow and ice melt and water runs into rivers

Rain falls on land and runs into rivers

Moisture in the air forms clouds

Clouds are moved by the wind

Rivers flow into the sea

Water evaporates from the sea

Moisture is taken into the air from the land, plants, animals, lakes and rivers

Some falls on the land and soaks into the ground or flows into streams and rivers. This continuous flow of water on land and in the air is called the water cycle.

When the rain falls, it replaces the water we have used. In fact, the water we use today is the same water that was drunk by the dinosaurs 250 million years ago. Nature has been **recycling** water since it first formed over 4 billion years ago.

*The water cycle allows us to use the same water over and over again.*

# Water to drink

Where does our drinking water come from? Some water comes from underground where it has collected in **aquifers**. These are rocks which hold water like a giant sponge. The water is pumped to the surface.

Some water is taken directly from rivers. The amount of water in rivers depends on how much rain has fallen. **Dams** are built across river valleys to collect water in **reservoirs**. This makes sure there is water available even if it does not rain for several weeks.

*Every person needs two litres of clean drinking water each day just to stay alive.*

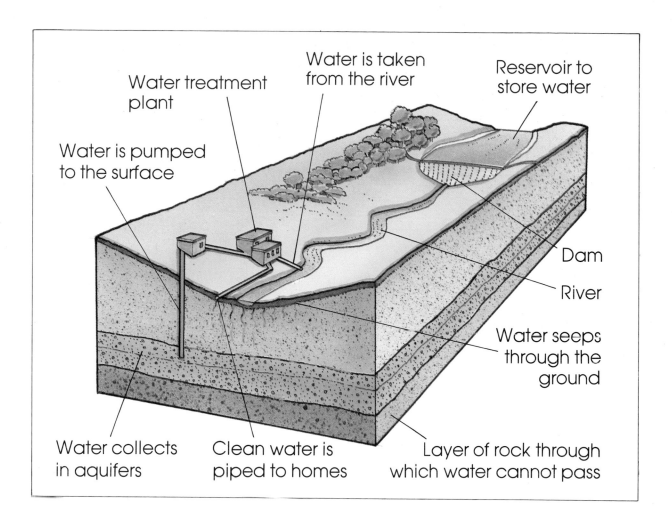

Water treatment plant

Water is taken from the river

Reservoir to store water

Water is pumped to the surface

Dam

River

Water seeps through the ground

Water collects in aquifers

Clean water is piped to homes

Layer of rock through which water cannot pass

The local **water company** then has to treat the water. It takes out unwanted bits like leaves and grit and makes sure the water does not contain harmful chemicals that may have got into it. **Chlorine** is added to kill any bugs that could make people ill. Once the water is clean enough to drink safely it goes into the water mains and from there to the buildings where people live and work.

• *The water supply for most people comes from lakes, reservoirs, rivers and under the ground.*

# Poor water supplies

Almost one third of people living in the world do not have a safe supply of water. The situation is worst in the poor countries of Africa, Asia and South America. Many people have to collect their water from ponds, streams and rivers which people also wash in and use as a toilet. Sometimes the water contains dangerous chemicals from factories and **sewage** from towns.

*Water from a well is usually safer to drink than water from a stream.*

Twenty five million people die every year because they are made ill by the water they drink or wash in. Poor people are affected worst of all because they cannot afford to buy clean water or build proper **sanitation**.

*These children in China use the river water to wash themselves, their vegetables and their pots and pans.*

The years 1981 to 1990 were the International Drinking Water Supply and Sanitation Decade. The **United Nations** hoped that by 1990 everyone would have a safe supply of water and proper sanitation. A lot of progress has been made, but millions of people are still made ill by the water they use.

# Water in the home

In developed countries, clean water from the **water supply plant** comes into the home through an underground pipe. Although it is all clean enough to drink, little of it is actually used for drinking.

Four people living in a house are likely to use over 500 litres of water a day. Imagine if you had to buy all that at the supermarket! What do we use it all for?

*Clean water comes into your home and dirty water goes out. How many different ways do you use water in the home?*

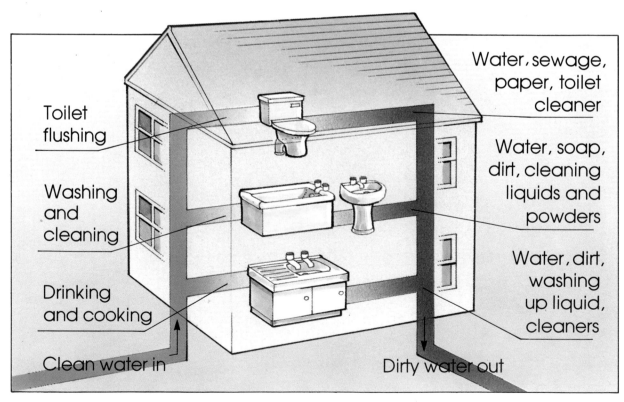

Toilet flushing

Washing and cleaning

Drinking and cooking

Clean water in

Water, sewage, paper, toilet cleaner

Water, soap, dirt, cleaning liquids and powders

Water, dirt, washing up liquid, cleaners

Dirty water out

*Water is used for removing dirt. We wash ourselves, clothes, windows, floors, cars and other things with water.*

Of every hundred litres used in the home, 27 are used for washing ourselves, 24 for flushing the toilet, 17 for washing clothes and 14 for washing dishes. Only 10 are used for cooking and drinking. The rest is used outside; for example, washing the car.

Once the water has been used it is no longer clean. It contains dirt, sewage and the many chemicals that are used in washing powders and other household cleaners. It must not mix with the clean water, so it goes out of the house by another pipe to the sewage works.

# Water for industry

Industries make things. Every product made, from a microchip to a steel girder, has used water. Industry is one of the main users of water. In the USA half of all the water used is consumed by industry. Why is so much water needed?

Water is used for cooling things because it absorbs a lot of heat and does not catch fire. It is used to cool engines in cars, lorries and ships. **Power stations** require enormous amounts of water for cooling.

*Great clouds of water vapour come from the cooling towers at a power station.*

*Left* Water is used in making many things we use everyday. Here it is added to flour and made into dough. This is then baked to make bread.

*Below* The waste going into this river in Britain can kill the plants and animals in it. This is called pollution.

A great deal of water is used in big factories where products are made. While factories use a lot of water, they also produce a lot of **waste**. Liquid waste is often mixed with water to **dilute** it, before being disposed of. If this waste is put into rivers or in the sea, it can kill the plants and animals that live there.

# Water on the farm

In many countries, most of the countryside is used by farmers to grow crops or feed animals. The rivers, streams and reservoirs which supply much of people's water are also found in the countryside. Farmers use a lot of water and they have to be careful that their dirty water does not escape and mix with the clean water supplies.

*These paddy fields in Japan are flooded with water while the rice plants grow.*

Farm animals also drink a lot of water. One cow drinks around 85 litres a day and produces about 13 litres of milk. The animals have to be washed and the animal houses cleaned out using water.

*This farmer in New Zealand mixes chemicals with water and sprays them over the plants.*

Modern farmers use a lot of poisonous chemicals which are mixed with water. Sheep are dipped in huge baths regularly to kill any **parasites** living on them. Fields are sprayed to kill weeds, and crops are sprayed to prevent damage by pests.

Some farmers have to water their crops to help them grow when the weather is very dry. This is called **irrigation**.

# Water for energy

*Moving water can be used to generate electricity. This is called hydroelectric power.*

Along the banks of some rivers and streams it is still possible to find **water mills**. People built them many years ago and used the water to drive a water wheel. As the wheel turned, it drove machines in the mill that were able to grind wheat into flour, drive **looms** to make cloth, or crush stones. There are very few working water mills left, but the power of moving water is used today to generate electricity.

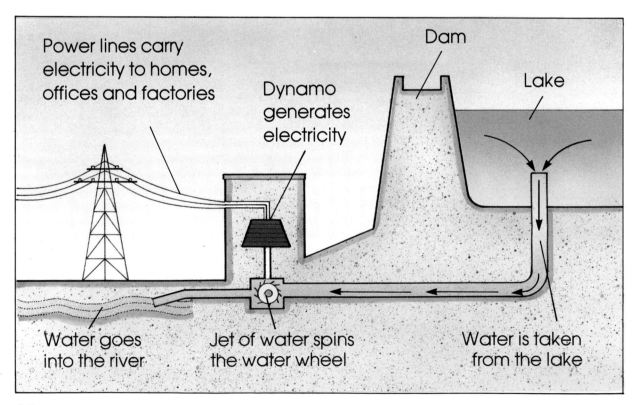

Power lines carry electricity to homes, offices and factories

Dynamo generates electricity

Dam

Lake

Water goes into the river

Jet of water spins the water wheel

Water is taken from the lake

A dam is built across a river valley. Water collects behind it and makes a lake. Water from the lake goes down a pipe and spins a wheel very rapidly. This wheel drives a **dynamo** which makes electricity. Electricity made in this way is called hydroelectric power.

The lakes are often popular tourist attractions. They can be used for sailing and fishing. They also attract a lot of water birds, like ducks and geese.

*The Hoover Dam in the USA holds back a great lake of water which is used to generate a lot of electricity.*

# Water for enjoyment

People get a lot of enjoyment from streams, rivers and lakes. They may enjoy a quiet walk in the countryside, or may come to watch the **wildlife**, to go fishing, swimming or sailing.

*This lake in Britain formed in an old gravel pit and is now used for water sports.*

Wildlife thrives in the countryside and in towns where there is clean water. In the water are many kinds of fish, insects and plants.

*An African fish eagle grabs a fish from the water in its powerful claws called talons.*

On the water are insects which skate on the surface and birds swimming around in search of food. Above the water, other birds skim the surface and catch insects. Some, like the kingfisher, dive into the water to catch fish. Animals live along the banks of rivers and streams.

Whenever we visit the countryside, we must leave it as we find it. If we drop litter, pick the flowers or make a lot of noise, we can upset the wildlife and make the place less enjoyable for other people.

*Fishing is a popular outdoor hobby, but fish cannot survive in polluted water.*

23

# Water gets dirty

All plants and animals, including people, need clean water to stay healthy. Clean rivers, lakes and seas are full of wildlife. When people make the water dirty, it is called **pollution**. Polluted water harms all living things.

The St Lawrence River in Canada is very polluted because many factories empty their waste into it. It has been the home of beluga whales for centuries, but now very few are left there.

*Rubbish that is thrown away carelessly makes places look ugly and can poison plants and animals.*

*This beluga, or white whale lives in the sea and like all animals needs clean water to live a healthy life.*

When the dead bodies of the whales are examined, they are found to be full of the harmful chemicals that pollute the river. Even popular bathing beaches, such as Bondi Beach in Australia, have to be closed because they get polluted with sewage.

Oil sometimes gets spilled onto water when there is an accident to a sea-going ship or **pipeline** that carries oil. The oil floats on the water and washes up on the coastline. Many birds and animals can die because of the oil, and it can take years to clean it all up.

*Oil spilled into the sea is washed up on the beaches. Cleaning up the oil is a dirty and difficult job.*

# Keeping water clean

To keep water clean, all the chemicals, sewage and other things that cause pollution must be kept away. Some dirty water is cleaned so it can be used again. Sewage works treat much of the waste water from the buildings where people live and work.

*This diagram shows how dirty water is cleaned at the sewage works before it is returned to the water cycle.*

The waste water goes along underground pipes to the sewage works. It passes through a screen which catches solid rubbish like plastic bags and bits of wood.

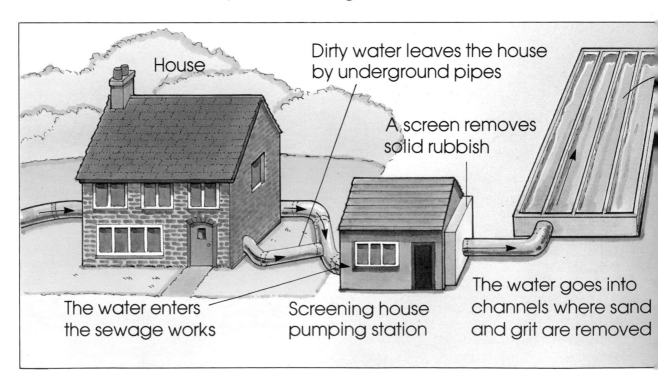

House

Dirty water leaves the house by underground pipes

A screen removes solid rubbish

The water enters the sewage works

Screening house pumping station

The water goes into channels where sand and grit are removed

It then runs slowly along channels. The sand and grit fall to the bottom and are collected. Next, the water goes into a large tank. Any tiny pieces of solid material sink to the bottom and are taken out.

The remaining water is either put into a large tank where air is blown through it, or sprinkled over stones in a large circular container. In both cases, tiny **organisms** feed on the dirt contained in the water until the water is clean enough to go back into the river.

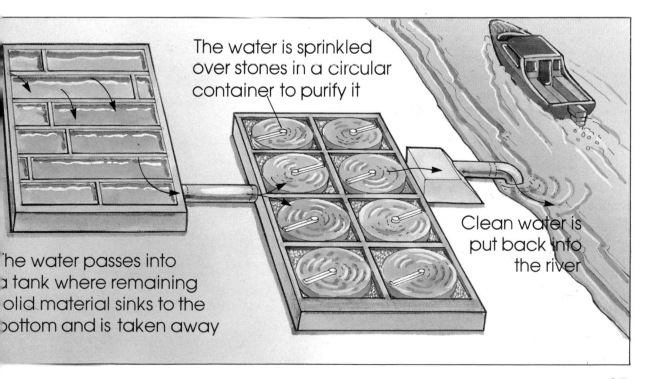

The water is sprinkled over stones in a circular container to purify it

The water passes into a tank where remaining solid material sinks to the bottom and is taken away

Clean water is put back into the river

# Projects with water

### Mini-water cycles

You will need:

A plastic bowl
Clear plastic bags or film

Large rubber bands
A small weight

1. Put about 2 cm of water in the bowl. Cover the top of the bowl with the plastic bag or film and seal it with a large rubber band.

2. Put a light weight in the centre of the plastic cover so it dips slightly in the middle. Put the bowl outside in the sun.

Can you see what happens as the sun warms the bowl? What happens when the water evaporates and cools?

3. You will also need a leafy plant.

Find out if a plant can produce water. Put a plastic bag over a leafy pot plant. Seal the bag with the rubber band. Leave it for a couple of days.

Describe what you see. What do you think has happened?

## How can we use less water?

You will need:

A timer with seconds                     Water tap
A bowl                                    A measuring jug

1. Measure how much water comes
from the tap in 5 seconds.

Catch the water in a bowl, and pour it
into the measuring jug.

2. As often as you can during the day, record how much water is used in your
home. Show the results in a table like this one:

Amount of water from the tap in 5 seconds = ½ Litre

| Time | Use of water | Number of seconds tap is on | Amount (Litres) |
|------|--------------|------------------------------|-----------------|
| 8.00 a.m. | Washing face and hands | 35 | 3½ |
| | Cleaning teeth | 30 | 3 |
| 8.15 a.m. | Filling kettle | 5 | ½ |
| 8.30 a.m. | Washing up | 120 | 12 |

From your results, decide with your family what you can do to use less water,
and by how much you can reduce the amount.

Repeat the survey from time to time to find out how well you are doing.

# Glossary

**Aquifers**   Rocks under the ground which have tiny spaces that contain water.

**Chlorine**   A chemical added to drinking water to kill harmful bugs.

**Dam**   A large structure built across a river to hold back the water.

**Dilute**   To reduce in strength by adding water.

**Dynamo**   A machine that makes electricity.

**Evaporate**   To turn water into a gas.

**Gas**   Any air-like substance that will take up the whole of the space that contains it.

**Irrigation**   A way of watering crops when there is not enough rainfall.

**Looms**   Machines used for weaving cloth.

**Organism**   A living creature or plant.

**Parasite**   A plant or animal that lives and feeds on another plant or animal.

**Pipeline**   A pipe used to carry gas, oil or water over a long distance.

**Pollution**   Damage to the environment caused by waste materials.

**Power station**   A place where electrical power is generated and distributed.

**Recycling**   Processing waste products so they can be used again.

**Reservoir**   A lake formed behind a dam to supply people with water.

**Sanitation**   The means by which sewage is kept separate from clean water.

**Sewage**   The waste water that goes down the sink or toilet.

**United Nations**   The international organization through which the countries of the world work together to solve world problems.

**Waste**   Things that have been used and are no longer required.

**Water company**   A company responsible for collecting water and providing clean water supplies.

**Water mills**   Factories where the machines are driven by water wheels.

**Water supply plant**   Where water supplies are cleaned and made fit for drinking.

**Wildlife**   Plants and animals that live wild.

# Books to read

Ardley, N. **Working with Water** (Franklin Watts, 1983)
Jennings, T. **Water** (Oxford University Press, 1982)
Satchwell, J. **Water** (Franklin Watts, 1985)
Sowter, N. **Water** (Souvenir, 1985)
Sowry, J. **Looking at Water** (Batsford, 1982)

**Useful addresses**

**Australia**
Water Resources Department
35 Spring Street
Melbourne, VIC 3000

The Snowy Mountains Hydro-Electric
    Authority
PO Box 332
Cooma, NSW 2630

**Canada**
Energy, Mines and Resources
Canada Communications Branch
55 St Clair Avenue East
Toronto
Ontario M4T 2PB

Ontario Hydro-Energy Information
700 University Avenue
Toronto
Ontario M5G 1X6

**New Zealand**
Water Resources Survey
Department of Scientific and
    Industrial Research
PO Box 29, 199
Christchurch

**UK**
National Rivers Authority
(Thames Region)
Kings Meadow House
Kings Meadow Road
Reading RG1 8DQ

Southern Water plc
Southern House
Yeoman Road
Worthing
West Sussex BN13 3NX

WaterAid
1 Queen Anne's Gate
London SW1H 9BT

# Index

## Picture acknowledgements

The publishers would like to thank the following for allowing their photographs to be reproduced in this book: Associated Press/Topham 8; Sally & Richard Greenhill 5 (bottom), 10, 13, 15, 21; J. Allan Cash Ltd 12, 17 (top), 24; Oxford Scientific Films 25 (top: Z. Leszczynski), (bottom: David Cayless); Seaphot Ltd: Planet Earth Pictures *cover* (top), 17 (bottom: Chris Howes), 22 (John and Gillian Lythgoe), 23 (Richard Coomber); Science Photo Library 5 (top: Tom van Sant/Geosphere Project, Santa Monica), 16 (Simon Fraser); Topham Picture Library 4; Wayland Picture Library *title page*, 7, 18, 19, 23 (bottom); ZEFA *cover* (bottom). The artwork was supplied by Stephen Wheele Design Associates.